CHARLES
DARWIN

CHARLES DARWIN

REVOLUTIONARY BIOLOGIST

J. Edward Evans

Lerner Publications Company • Minneapolis

Library of Congress Cataloging-in-Publication Data

Evans, J. Edward.
    Charles Darwin : revolutionary biologist / by J. Edward Evans.
        p.   cm.
    Includes bibliographical references (p.   ) and index.
    Summary: A biography of the English naturalist who, after collecting plants and animals from around the world, came up with the theory of evolution by natural selection.
    ISBN 0-8225-4914-X
    1. Darwin, Charles, 1809-1882—Juvenile literature. 2. Naturalists—England—Biography—Juvenile literature. [1. Darwin, Charles, 1809-1882. 2. Naturalists.]
I. Title.
QH31.D2E93   1993
575'.0092—dc20
[B]   92-45281
                                                                                             CIP
                                                                                             AC

Manufactured in the United States of America

1 2 3 4 5 6 98 97 96 95 94 93

472557

Contents

Charles Darwin

⚐ ONE ⚐

The Hidden Tremor
1858-1859

The president of the Linnean Society of London walked out of the society's meeting on July 1, 1858, lamenting that no gems of knowledge had been unearthed during the past year. "The year has not, indeed, been marked by any of those striking discoveries which at once revolutionize, so to speak, the departments of science on which they bear."

Papers written by Charles Darwin and Alfred Russell Wallace had been read by the society's secretary at the meeting, but no one took any notice. The papers outlined a theory of evolution—that existing species of plants and animals changed over the generations. A few brash French and English scientists had been bringing up the subject of evolution with increasing frequency for the past 60 years. A number of wild theories had been proposed, never with any concrete evidence. These latest works by Darwin and Wallace were widely considered to be more of the same, a rehashing of old ideas sprinkled with a few reckless new notions.

During the meeting, Charles and Emma Darwin were burying their youngest son, who had died from scarlet fever.

Their grief was profound. Yet it was almost overshadowed by looming fears of an epidemic. At the same time, Charles's fears of public controversy over his paper were mounting. He had spent the past 20 years collecting, arranging, and rearranging his data. Now, at the meeting of the Linnean Society, he was finally making public his theory on the evolution of species through a phenomenon called "the survival of the fittest."

Scarcely more than a year later, Darwin published a book, *On the Origin of Species by Means of Natural Selection.*

Cartoonists had a field day with Darwin, shown here as promoting cruelty to animals with his theories on the descent of human beings from lower primates.

Another cartoon of Darwin, accusing him of making "a contribution to unnatural history"

The ideas he expressed in this book shook the foundations of Western society. Some people found his writings so upsetting, yet so persuasive, that they were convinced his theories signaled the end of civilization. Even those who doubted Darwin's theory recognized that he had set off a scientific revolution that would permanently alter the way people looked at the world.

Contemporaries of Charles Darwin watched in bewilderment as this amateur scientist devised theories that for centuries had eluded the finest minds in the world. The concept of evolution now seemed so simple to many of them, so obvious. "How stupid not to have thought of it before!" exclaimed English biologist Thomas H. Huxley, after reading Darwin's ideas.

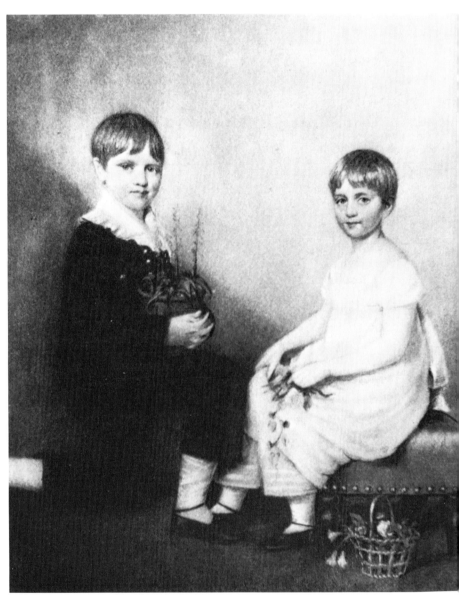

Charles and his sister Emily Catherine, painted here in 1816, were raised by their older sister Caroline, who thought of Charles as "particularly affectionate, tractable & sweet-tempered."

✠ TWO ✠

The Young Gentleman
1809-1825

Charles Darwin was the grandson of Erasmus Darwin, a famous English physician who brought fame as well as fortune to the Darwin family. Born in 1731, Erasmus graduated from medical school and set out to establish a practice in the town of Lichfield. Few patients were willing to entrust their health to the new doctor, however, until a young gentleman came to him in desperation. All of the other doctors in the area had diagnosed the gentleman's condition as being beyond help. Erasmus, however, managed to cure the ailment with a novel method of treatment.

News of the incident spread quickly, and Erasmus instantly gained fame as an expert. His reputation eventually grew to such an extent that he was offered a position as King George III's personal physician. Erasmus declined the honor and instead pursued a variety of ambitions. He was proud of his poetry, which was in demand nearly as much as his medical skill.

In 1794 Erasmus published *Zoonomia: The Laws of Organic Life*, which was primarily a medical textbook.

*Erasmus
Darwin,
Charles's
grandfather*

Erasmus was a religious freethinker and a member of the
Lunar Society—a group of intellectuals and political radicals
who supported the American colonists' struggle for inde-
pendence, opposed slavery, and believed in reason rather
than orthodox religion.

Erasmus Darwin was a charitable man; he never charged
his poorer patients for his services. Yet he was prosperous.
He also increased the family's social standing when he be-
friended Josiah Wedgwood. Josiah was even more famous for

manufacturing his fine pottery than Dr. Darwin was for his medicine. A Unitarian, Josiah was slightly more religious than Erasmus, but still a fairly radical thinker. Josiah established an innovative school for his own children, which Erasmus's children also attended.

The close friendship of Erasmus and Josiah led to the marriage of Erasmus's son Robert to Josiah's oldest daughter, Susannah, in 1796—a year after Josiah's death. Susannah brought an ample inheritance with her when she joined Robert at his home in Shrewsbury, near the Welsh border. She also brought her Unitarian faith, although the second generation of Darwins and Wedgwoods conformed more to the traditional Anglican religion than their fathers did. Her children would be baptized Anglican and brought up to believe, as did most of the people in England, that human beings were created in the image of God and had little in common with the rest of creation.

Robert Darwin proved that he could succeed without financial help from either his father or his wife's family. Robert started his own medical practice with a very small amount of money and built it up to a comfortable business.

In 1798, Susannah gave birth to their first child, Marianne. Marianne was followed by Caroline, born in 1800; Susan, born in 1803; Erasmus, born in 1804; and Charles Robert, born on February 12, 1809. One year after Charles's birth, Emily Catherine was born. Susannah had had a difficult pregnancy with Caroline, and by the time Charles was born, she was practically an invalid. Even so, Susannah maintained her interest in gardening. She taught Charles how to remember the names of plants by looking at their flowers.

Robert Darwin was an enormous man. He stood about 6 feet, 2 inches tall and weighed over 350 pounds. When he

The imposing Dr. Robert Darwin in 1839

was visiting a patient, he would send a coachman ahead to test the sturdiness of the stairs. A serious man, Dr. Darwin felt it was his duty to finish the day with a stern lecture to his children. For up to two hours, he spelled out his demands and expectations. There was, of course, no argument. Whenever Robert Darwin walked into a gathering, all conversation immediately stopped. Young Charles, along with all his brothers and sisters, respected his domineering father. In his later letters, he never referred to his father without adding, "who is the wisest man I ever knew" or, "who was the kindest man I ever knew."

As a boy, Charles was caught between the expectations of his father on one hand, and the strict supervision of his sister Caroline on the other. Caroline took it upon herself to fill the role of mother to Charles. But in Charles's eyes, her mothering consisted chiefly of correcting anything about his behavior that she did not like.

Charles loved the outdoors. He later described himself as a born naturalist. He enjoyed catching glimpses of wild birds and other animals that lived along the River Severn, which flowed past the Darwin house. Gardening, collecting

Charles's birthplace and childhood home in Shrewsbury

rocks, hunting for seashells, and fishing for newts took up as much of his time as he could spare. He was so good with dogs that he could coax almost any dog away from its master. His own dog, Polly, was so devoted to him that she would sulk whenever he went away from the house.

Charles also looked forward to the frequent family visits to Maer, the home of the Wedgwoods, 20 miles away. Compared to the atmosphere at home, life among Charles's cousins was relaxed and free. Among them he could enjoy pleasant company and genuine two-way conversation. The lakes and deep woods of Maer provided an even more beautiful natural playground than Charles enjoyed at Shrewsbury.

Shrewsbury as seen from the River Severn

In the spring of 1817, Charles was sent to a Unitarian day school. He was a sweet-natured boy whose only noticeable fault was a tendency to tell lies. Most of these were so harmless that they seem to have brought more smiles than punishments from his father. Once Charles claimed that he was able to produce brightly colored flowers in his garden by watering them with colored liquid. Another time he secretly picked fruit from the family garden and hid it. Then he led his family to the fruit that he had "discovered" and declared that it was the stash of a thief who had stolen it from them.

Charles himself could be a gullible target of pranks. Once a friend informed him that a bakery was giving away free cakes to anyone who walked into the store with his hat cocked at a certain angle. Charles arranged his hat in the proper fashion, walked into the store, and collected his cakes. When he left without paying for them, he was chased by an angry baker, much to the amusement of Charles's friend.

Susannah Darwin died in 1817 when Charles was only eight. Charles once admitted that he could remember nothing about her except for her work table and a few ornaments that had decorated her funeral.

In 1818 Dr. Darwin enrolled Charles, along with his brother, Erasmus, in the Shrewsbury Grammar School. Although the Darwins lived only a mile from the school, the boys lived there as boarders. Nine-year-old Charles shared a bed with Erasmus.

The Shrewsbury Grammar School had once been considered one of the finer schools in England. Its reputation had since declined before being rescued by a young schoolmaster, Samuel Butler. Butler had brought back the school's good reputation with a simple back-to-the-basics formula. At the time, education for boys was to consist almost entirely

Shrewsbury Grammar School

of learning the classics, Greek and Latin, by rote memory and recitation. The more that the boys who would grow up to be gentlemen knew about ancient cultures, the English believed, the more they had command of their own culture. On Sundays the boys studied the Bible.

When left to himself after school, Charles would often sit in a window of the thick-walled school, reading the plays of Shakespeare. He also organized impressive, orderly collections of shells, coins, rocks, and minerals. He and his brother even set up their own chemistry laboratory in a toolshed at their home. Like other boys of his age and social standing, he learned to hunt. He threw himself into the sport with a passion. For Charles, the rote learning of Greek and Latin was completely dull.

Neither Charles nor his teacher had much respect for each other. Dr. Butler had given his student a public scolding for wasting his time on such frivolous things as chemistry experiments. He considered Charles to be lazy and only an ordinary student at best.

For his part, Charles did not believe that he was learning anything of value at the Shrewsbury Grammar School. But Robert Darwin agreed with Dr. Butler. In anger, Robert fumed that Charles cared for nothing but shooting, dogs, and rat-catching, and he predicted the boy would never amount to anything.

Dr. Darwin pulled Charles out of the school when his son was 16 and sent him to medical school. Medicine was a respectable occupation, and Charles had shown at least some interest in the field. He had even collected a half dozen patients of his own—poor women and children of Shrewsbury. Charles carefully recorded the symptoms of their ailments and described them to his father. Dr. Darwin offered advice concerning treatment, and Charles formulated the medicines himself.

Edinburgh University, in Scotland, offered the finest medical training in Great Britain at that time. In October 1825, Charles was sent there to join his brother, Erasmus, who was beginning his final year of medical school. Charles found the lectures, except those on chemistry, unbearably boring. While watching a surgeon perform an operation on a child—without anesthesia—Charles became so upset that he bolted out of the room. Never again would he set foot in an operating room.

Having lost interest in a medical career, Charles put no effort into his studies. He secretly decided that his father was wealthy enough to provide both of his sons with a comfortable living. That summer he hiked through the Welsh hills. After reading Gilbert White's *The Natural History of Selborne,* Charles began studying the habits of birds. He learned to treat birds less like hunting targets and more as a scientific curiosity, carefully observing their habits and writing down his observations.

That summer he also read his grandfather's medical textbook, *Zoonomia.* In the middle of the book, Erasmus had approached the subject of evolution. Erasmus had studied the changes that take place in animals as they grow from an embryo to an adult. He noticed that markedly different adult animals look very much alike in their early stages. Nature's ability to take two similar embryos and fashion them into such different shapes seemed to indicate something about the ability of animals to change or adapt to different situations.

Erasmus had also noted that certain desirable traits, such as strength and speed, could be bred into dogs and horses over generations. This proved that, over time, the characteristics of a species could be changed. Perhaps great numbers of changes had occurred in species throughout the earth's history. Was it not possible, Erasmus had asked, that a great many species of animals came from a single "living filament," as he had called it?

A view of Edinburgh Castle on the hill overlooking the city of Edinburgh, where Charles was sent by his father to study medicine

Unfortunately, Erasmus's ideas on evolution were not supported by scientific evidence. While such creative dreaming was important in opening up new possibilities, it was hardly grounds for proposing a new scientific theory. Nevertheless, Charles was quite impressed by the argument.

From the time he was a young boy, Charles collected rocks, sea-shells, and hunting trophies. At Cambridge he became interested in beetles and promptly began to collect them. Here Charles is shown "beetling" in a sketch by a friend.

THREE

The Compulsive Collector
1826-1831

With his brother now graduated from Edinburgh, 17-year-old Charles was left to fend for himself during his second year of medical school. During that year, he found others who shared his interest in nature. He joined two other young men, Robert Grant and John Coldstream, for long walks in the woods. They frequently collected small creatures from the tide pools and brought them home for dissection.

During one of their excursions into the woods, Grant spoke highly of Jean Baptiste de Lamarck and his arguments on evolution. As Charles listened, he noticed that Lamarck's views sounded very much like those of his grandfather.

Early in the 19th century, any ideas concerning evolution were condemned by the Anglican church and by scientific authorities as morally corrupt and subversive. But a number of European scientists had discussed evolution in previous centuries; some of them had been imprisoned and even executed for their views.

M. le CHEVALIER de LAMARCK,
Professor of Botany of the National Institute.

In the 18th century, Comte de Buffon, a French scientist, had concluded that life on earth had probably undergone considerable changes from the time it had been created. According to Buffon, animals must have the ability to adapt to their environment. If they did not, they could not have survived, nor could they continue to survive.

In his book *Philosophie Zoologique*, written in 1809, Jean Baptiste de Lamarck declared that Buffon had been on the right track. All that Buffon had lacked was a reasonable explanation of *how* animals evolved. Lamarck thought he understood how these physical changes in animals took place. He argued that the direction of evolution depended on the wishes and needs of the animals, which varied with the environment in which the animal lived. In other words, the environment could shape animals into a form that would best enable them to cope with their surroundings.

For example, a bird that gathered its food by wading in the water had a need for longer legs than did the average bird. Therefore, wading in the water would, over a period of time, cause the wading bird's legs to lengthen. Similarly, in

In his theories on species development, Lamarck concluded that a wading bird, like this, had lengthened its legs to better suit its environment.

their efforts to reach leaves on tall trees, giraffes had been able to stretch their necks farther and farther until they had reached their present length. Extremely cold weather must have caused some mammals to grow thick fur. Lamarck also theorized that traits an animal no longer needed would eventually disappear. If giraffes lived in a place where trees were very short, their necks would gradually shorten.

By the time Charles was in medical school, Lamarck's theory and all other theories of evolution had been rejected by most scientists. The prevailing view was that each species had been created by God as it was, and each remained unchanged from the beginning of time to the 19th century. The religious climate in England made it difficult to put much stock in evolution. Unlike France, where the scientific community operated almost as if the church did not exist, English scientists were often clergymen. Whereas some French scientists had no qualms about attacking the church, English scientists, at the very least, tried to operate within the rules laid down by church officials.

None of these ideas on evolution, however, were of any use to a medical student. By the end of his second year, it was obvious even to his father that Charles was not cut out to be a physician. Dr. Darwin was near his wit's end trying to find a profession for the young man. The only profession for which Charles seemed remotely suited was the clergy. The Anglican church was corrupt, complacent, and wealthy. Any gentleman unsuited for another profession could buy a country parish, with a few acres to farm, and continue pursuing any hobbies he chose.

As usual, Charles went along with his father's plans.

Satisfied that there was nothing in the doctrine of the Anglican church that bothered his conscience, he prepared to study theology. Ironically, the study of theology required a comprehensive understanding of Greek and Latin, subjects that had bored Charles at Shrewsbury. So after intense refresher courses in Greek and Latin, he set off for Christ's College at Cambridge in 1828.

The atmosphere at Christ's College was perfectly suited to young Charles's taste. Most of the students were the privileged sons of well-to-do country gentlemen. A likable young man, Charles was easily swept along with the revelry that such a group enjoyed. He spent many of his days hunting or

A drawing of the view from the tobacconist's where Charles first lodged in Cambridge

riding horseback with his friends, or looking at paintings in the Fitzwilliam Museum. In the evening, these friends would often gather for dinner and follow the meal with a night of drinking, cardplaying, and laughter.

There was nothing that Charles found so enjoyable and relaxing as going out into the woods to shoot partridge. He became an expert marksman because of his great attention to detail. He drilled himself repeatedly in front of a mirror,

The Mill Pond in Cambridge. Charles hired a collector to scour the bottoms of barges for beetles.

making sure that he always threw the barrel of his gun up at the same precise height. He also kept a detailed record of every bird he shot.

The night before going hunting, Charles would leave his boots ready next to his bed. Despite the fact that he would be spending the entire day in the woods, he could not bear to lose half a minute in gathering his boots in the morning.

At the same time, Charles was developing a fascination with insects. His second cousin, William Darwin Fox, had steered Charles's natural passion for collecting toward beetles. The cousins frequently wrote to compare notes on their collections. Charles became so consumed by collecting beetles that he once wrote to William that he was dying by inches from not having anyone to talk to about insects.

While he was on a hike during a holiday in northern Wales, Charles happened upon two huge poisonous snakes. He killed the snakes and quickly buried them to attract beetles. A week later, he returned to collect the beetles.

On another occasion, Charles found three rare species of beetles in one place. Rather than risk losing any of them, he placed one of the beetles in his mouth and carried the others in each hand. Unfortunately, the beetle in his mouth protected itself by spraying a fluid that burned Charles's mouth so badly he was forced to spit out the beetle.

Charles was not shy about overspending the allowance given him by his father. He paid a man to scrape moss from trees in the winter and to search garbage barrels for rare species of insects. He even hired choirboys to sing to him in his rooms. All of this cost a considerable amount of money.

His busy social life left him little time or energy for his studies. Charles rated his educational experience at Christ's College equal to his other attempts at learning. "My time was wasted, as far as the academic studies were concerned, as completely as at Edinburgh and at school." Showing his usual impatience with anything that did not fascinate him, he got average marks and did the minimum amount of work necessary to earn his degree. Looking back on those three years, Charles later remarked that he should have been ashamed of himself. Yet he could not help but confess that they were the most joyful three years of his life.

Even though Charles accomplished little in his formal education, his pursuit of his hobbies laid the groundwork for his future career. Through his brother, he heard of John Stevens Henslow, an enthusiastic professor of botany at Cambridge. The two men met and became close friends. They frequently spent long afternoons in the woods, discussing plants. According to Charles, Henslow knew a great deal about botany, entomology, chemistry, mineralogy, and geology. His strongest suit was to draw conclusions from long-continued observations. Since Henslow was a clergyman as well as a professor of botany, his example offered some hope that Charles could combine his interest in science with his profession as a clergyman.

Scientists and clergy alike believed that the world was a finished product. The earth still looked the same as it had since creation. Mountains stood where they had been placed by God, seas covered the areas they had always covered. The animals that roamed the earth looked the same as their ancestors did when they were created at the beginning of time.

Both the book of Genesis and the ideas of the Greek philosopher Plato seemed to support this point of view. Plato described changes and variations in real things as being imperfect defects from the original "perfect" form. Thus, the original world was the "perfect" world. The idea that nature

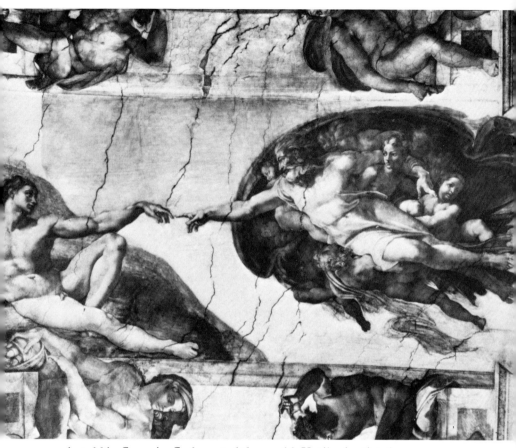

As told in Genesis, God created the world. Until scientists began to think about evolution, most Europeans believed that the world was created perfect and unchangeable. Shown here is The Creation of Adam, *painted by Michelangelo on the ceiling of the Sistine Chapel in 1511. Adam is portrayed as the pinnacle of God's creation.*

would ever alter itself from its original, perfect form seemed laughable—and blasphemous.

This fundamental belief in an unchanging, perfectly created world had gone unchallenged until rock collectors in the 17th century began to uncover some disturbing evidence:

fossils. Careful examination showed that fossils were not merely interesting patterns etched in stone. They were the remains of once-living things. Some of these fossils were from creatures and plants that no one had ever seen alive. Obviously, then, the idea that nothing had changed since creation was faulty. If some of the creatures that once lived on the earth no longer existed, then the world had changed and was not the same perfect one that God created.

So people used the biblical story of Noah's flood to explain the changing earth. A few thousand years ago, at the time of the flood, the sea rose and wiped out much of life on the earth. But geologists then discovered places where separate layers of rock each contained fossils of extinct life. The separate layers of rock apparently were formed at different times, and so there must have been a number of great catastrophes like the flood that had wiped out life forms on earth.

With this understanding of fossils in mind, Charles accompanied a friend of Henslow's, geology professor Adam Sedgwick, on a geological expedition after finishing his studies at Christ's College in the summer of 1831. The expedition was in northern Wales, not far from Charles's home. While on the tour, Charles discovered a tropical mollusk shell in the hands of a local workman. The man explained that he had found the shell in a nearby gravel pit. According to Sedgwick, the shell could not possibly have been in temperate, non-tropical, Wales. If it had been, he said that it would be the greatest misfortune to geology, as it would overthrow all that geologists know. Charles was thrilled to discover such an unexpected and important piece of geological evidence. Sedgwick, however, did not share Charles's excitement. Instead he seemed irritated by people finding evidence that upset the accepted theories.

Adam Sedgwick

The professor's resistance to a piece of new data made a lasting impression on Charles. It served to reinforce a feeling of embarrassment that Charles had recently felt about the works of his grandfather. In rereading Erasmus Darwin's *Zoonomia,* Charles was newly critical of all the speculation that was included among the facts. In many matters of science, Erasmus had made guesses about the truth, without bothering to cite any evidence. As he became more involved in science, Charles Darwin remembered his grandfather speculating without evidence and Sedgwick resisting the evidence. Fearful of repeating their mistakes, he put off drawing conclusions from his evidence as long as possible.

The hills of Wales, where Charles participated in a geological expedition with Adam Sedgwick

◢◣ FOUR ◥◤

A New Opportunity
1831-1832

Robert Darwin was not quite sure why his son, at the age of 22, was wandering through the Welsh countryside with Adam Sedgwick. Dr. Darwin had little appreciation for science, a profession not considered to be legitimate by the English nobility. Charles had finished his schooling at Christ's College in Cambridge and was still more interested in natural history and science than in the church. In fact, Charles was even more focused on hunting than science. At the end of August 1831, Charles left the Sedgwick expedition early so that he could get back to his cousins' home in time for partridge hunting.

On his way to Maer, he stopped at home in Shrewsbury for the night. There he found a letter waiting for him. Captain Robert FitzRoy, of the HMS *Beagle*, was looking for a naturalist and companion to sail along with him on a surveying trip—originally planned to take three years—of the southern and western coasts of South America. FitzRoy's expeditions were thorough and productive, and he insisted on assembling a first-class crew. He preferred to hire qualified naturalists and geologists to document the plants, animals, and minerals of South America's coasts.

FitzRoy already had a naturalist assigned to his crew. In approaching Charles, he was not as much interested in hiring a second naturalist as he was in simply finding someone to keep himself company. Because FitzRoy came from an illustrious family, custom dictated that his companion must be a gentleman. Also, while room and board would be provided, this gentleman would have to finance his own work. The cost of gathering, storing, and shipping specimens over at least three years was greater than the average naturalist could afford.

Professor Henslow had recommended his student and hiking partner, Charles Darwin. Even though Charles had no formal training as a naturalist, Henslow said, he had shown great interest in the natural sciences, he was a world-class collector, and he enjoyed being outdoors. Moreover, Charles came from a respectable, well-to-do family and seemed to be extremely likable.

When Charles opened the letter asking if he was interested in sailing with the *Beagle,* he considered the offer a dream come true. Along with his love of the outdoors, his interest in natural history had been aroused by several books that he had recently read about the fascinating variety of life in the tropics.

Dr. Robert Darwin, however, was not impressed. He listed his objections, including his beliefs that natural history was not a worthwhile calling, that the trip would be a waste of valuable years, that once Charles had gained a taste for such adventures he would never settle down, that it was a wild and reckless scheme, and that Charles would be delaying—if not abandoning—his profession as a clergyman. That night, he wrote a letter declining the offer.

The next day, Charles went to Maer. While staying with the Wedgwoods, he mentioned the offer to them. The Wedgwoods were astounded to hear that Charles had turned his back on such an opportunity. Charles's uncle Josiah quickly approached Robert and argued away every one of his objections. Josiah reminded him that natural history was an important area of study for an Anglican clergyman and that years at sea often made men more eager to settle down once they returned home.

Dr. Darwin changed his mind, and Charles rushed off to try to undo the effects of his letter. In early September, Captain FitzRoy summoned Charles to London for an interview with him to see if the two were compatible.

As he met with FitzRoy, Charles had no idea how closely the captain was examining him. As Charles heard the story later, FitzRoy believed that a person's character could be judged by the shape and size of his nose. Charles's wide, flattened nose indicated to the captain that this new recruit would not be able to endure a long voyage.

After talking to the young man, however, FitzRoy decided that perhaps there was more to Darwin than his nose seemed to indicate. He displayed charm and personality, and he appeared strong enough to survive physical hardship. Charles, in turn, found the captain to be capable and likable, although a bit quirky.

The next step was for Charles to find out more about his prospective voyage. On October 25, 1831, he traveled south to the port of Plymouth to inspect the *Beagle*. The *Beagle* was an older type of brig known as, in the grim humor of British naval slang, a "coffin" because of a tendency to sink in bad weather. The 10-gun vessel was only 90 feet in length. For the next three years, assuming the ship stayed afloat,

Charles would have to share this overcrowded space with 74 crew members. Charles's quarters were spacious compared to those of most of the crew, but even he had just room in which to turn around. Captain FitzRoy assured Charles that he would not be trapped aboard the ship for three years. The ship would anchor in many ports, he said, and Charles could ask to be sent home at any time.

FitzRoy had originally planned to set sail in late September. But the ship was undergoing major repairs, and these delays were followed by a long stretch of rough weather that postponed the *Beagle*'s departure.

A few days before the launch, Charles was frightened by a strange and irregular rhythm of his heartbeat. Even though he was certain he had a heart disease, he refused to see a doctor. After all the close calls that had nearly prevented him from making the trip, he would not risk having a doctor declare him unfit to travel.

Finally, on December 27, 1831, the HMS *Beagle* set sail. As Charles had feared, the pitching and rocking of the boat brought on an attack of seasickness almost at once. Throughout his voyage on the *Beagle*, Charles never fully adjusted to the constantly rolling waves. Many times he would attempt to work, only to be driven to his cot by bouts of nausea after less than an hour of effort.

After the monotony of sailing for two months with nothing to do, many of the sailors had turned to drinking to make the boredom more bearable. Captain FitzRoy had the offending sailors whipped and put in chains. Charles, who could not stand cruelty of any kind, was very upset. He soon found that his thinking was so different from FitzRoy's on so many subjects that fulfilling his role as captain's companion would be as difficult as any challenge he faced on the trip.

Shark fishing from the prow of the Beagle

Fortunately, Charles knew how to converse with opinion-ated people such as the captain without upsetting them. Although there were tense moments, Charles managed to

The Voyage of the Beagle around South America 1831-1836

TO ENGLAND

Equator

GALAPAGOS
ISLANDS

ECUADOR

TO
NEW
ZEALAND

PERU

Lima

BRAZIL

Pernambuco
(Recife)

A
N
D
E
S

PACIFIC
OCEAN

Rio de
Janeiro

CHILE

URUGUAY

ATLANTIC
OCEAN

Santiago

Buenos
Aires

Montevideo

Concepción

ARGENTINA

FALKLAND
ISLANDS

TIERRA
DEL
FUEGO

CHILE

TIERRA
DEL
FUEGO

Strait of
Magellan

Beagle
Canal

MT. SARMIENTO

N
W   E
S

hold his tongue. Most of the time he simply avoided arguing about the captain's favorite issues.

There were exceptions to his silence, however, and they were most often over the issue of slavery. Charles's grandfather Erasmus had been outspoken in his opposition to slavery. This heritage, along with Charles's passionate hatred of cruelty, combined to put him squarely at odds with the aristocratic FitzRoy.

Charles had far more respect for Africans than did most Europeans or Americans of his time. While a student at Edinburgh, he had ignored the conventions of high society and had made friends with an African taxidermist. During the course of their friendship, Charles learned how to stuff and mount birds and other game.

The captain, however, had little regard for the African race, and he strongly defended slavery as being in the best interests of all parties concerned. He once told Charles of a visit he had made to a slave owner in Brazil. In the captain's presence, the man had brought in his slaves one at a time to ask them if they wished to be free. Each had replied that he or she was happier being a slave.

For once, Charles's strong feelings overcame his reluctance to cause trouble. He pointed out to the captain, with a hint of a sneer, that one could hardly expect a slave to say anything else in front of his or her master.

No one was supposed to talk to a captain of a British ship that way. FitzRoy flew into a rage. He declared that he could no longer share his quarters or his table with someone who doubted his word. But Charles was welcomed to the table of other crewmembers. A few hours later, FitzRoy's temper had calmed. He sought out Charles, apologized, and asked him to come back.

The Beagle *sailing through the Strait of Magellan, with Mount Sarmiento in the background*

✍ FIVE 🖊

A Fateful Voyage

1832-1833

In preparing Charles for his research in South America, Professor Henslow had tried to make certain that Charles was aware of the latest writings in natural history and geology. One of the books he had recommended was *Principles of Geology* by Charles Lyell, a geologist from Scotland. Henslow warned Charles that Lyell proposed some dangerous theories in the book. But if one could ignore those, a great deal of useful information could be gained from reading it.

With plenty of time on his hands during the ocean voyage, Charles pored over the first volume, and then was overjoyed to receive Lyell's recently published second volume from Henslow during his first year on the *Beagle*. Instead of rejecting Lyell's more radical proposals, as he had been advised to do, Charles found them fascinating.

In *Principles of Geology*, Lyell described what he thought was a far more logical explanation of the layers of fossils than the notion that God was repeatedly destroying and re-creating creatures. Lyell believed that the earth was slowly and continually being changed. Wind, rain, volcanoes, earthquakes, and changing climates combined to rearrange the earth. If such changes were drastic enough, they could make parts of the earth unlivable for some of the plants and animals that had previously lived there. This process would cause creatures to die out slowly and naturally, rather than by a long series of disasters.

The ideas of mountains growing and wearing down and of climates changing seemed farfetched to most people. Such changes, if they happened, took place too slowly for people to observe them. In order for Lyell's argument to make sense, the earth had to be many thousands, perhaps even millions, of years old.

This was exactly what Lyell claimed, and it was this argument that appalled many educated people. Church officials used the Bible to calculate that the earth had been created less than 6,000 years earlier. The claim that the earth was hundreds of thousands of years old seemed contrary to common sense, as well as to all religious teaching.

By accepting Lyell's judgment that the earth was many times older than commonly believed and was in a constant state of change, Charles kept finding himself confronted with the knotty issue of evolution. If the earth was constantly changing, the environment in which animals lived was constantly changing. If species of plants and animals were unable to adapt to these changes in their environment, then they would die. If that were the case, how could one explain the enormous variety of living things on the earth?

The most logical explanation for the existence of a variety of life in a changing world seemed to be that old forms of plants and animals must have died out and been replaced by new forms. The first part of that explanation was supported by the fossil records. Some types of plants and animals had become extinct. Presumably, then, new forms must also be appearing, otherwise the numbers of creatures on earth would be rapidly diminishing.

The next and most intriguing question to Charles was, how were the old forms replaced? For an English scientist of the time, and especially for one who had been planning to be an Anglican clergyman, there was supposed to be only one answer to this question. All species of plants and animals were created by God as finished products. If some species had indeed died out and been replaced, they had been re-placed by separate acts of creation.

The Charles Darwin who read Lyell's arguments while sailing toward adventure was basically a loyal supporter of the traditional church view. Before deciding on a career as

The Beagle *had to be laid ashore for repairs in southern Argentina.*

This engraving of Brazil's rain forest prompted Charles to visit the tropics.

clergyman, he had studied the teachings of the church and had found them acceptable. Early in his journey aboard the *Beagle,* Charles held to his orthodox beliefs so firmly that the crew made fun of him. Even the more devout crew members were amused by the way Darwin tried to settle every argument with a quote from the Bible. But the more Charles thought about Lyell's theories, and he had plenty of spare time in which to think, the more fascinating they became.

When the *Beagle* landed on the coast of South America, Charles found himself surrounded by a breathtaking beauty far beyond his expectations. He could hardly contain himself amid the exotic splendor of this tropical paradise. He recognized that he had been given a chance few would ever receive. A virtually unmapped continent lay at his feet. The slow prowling of the *Beagle* as FitzRoy gathered surveying data along the coast would give Charles plenty of time to make detailed studies.

Charles felt incredibly free when he reached shore and began his work. Until he left England, Charles had hardly been able to take a step without feeling the weight of his proud father's expectations on him. And on this voyage, he had been burdened by his role as companion to the eccentric and opinionated Captain FitzRoy.

With Robert Darwin thousands of miles away and Captain FitzRoy busy surveying the coast, Charles found himself in the middle of a natural wonderland, free from any supervisor or authority. With no specific instructions, he could decide for himself what his job was and how he wanted to do it.

Much of his task, it seemed to him, was to do the very things that he had always loved: hunting, collecting, and exploring. Spurred on by the excitement of discovering new wildlife, Charles took on these tasks with even more than his usual gusto. During FitzRoy's survey of South America's eastern coast, Charles did almost all of his work by himself. Whenever he saw a new form of animal life, he shot it and

An artist's rendering of Charles examining fossils in South America

added it to his collection. Charles claimed to have shot as many as 80 different species of birds on a single morning walk. He once found approximately 68 new species of beetles in one day. When confined to the ship, he managed to catch marine animals for dissection.

But even his fascination with collecting diverse forms of animal life did not shake Lyell's theories from his mind. When Charles discovered numerous fossils in Brazil and Argentina, he immediately thought of Lyell's *Principles of Geology*. Lyell was not some bookish professor spouting abstract theories; he had made a serious attempt to explain changes in species of plants and animals. Charles was digging supporting evidence right out of the soil.

Charles was captivated not only by Lyell's arguments but also by his method of argument. Charles tried to follow Lyell's example of developing a working hypothesis, collecting evidence, then examining the evidence to see if the hypothesis held up or needed to be changed.

Desperate to uncover more evidence in support of what Lyell had written, Charles began collecting even more samples. Along with his sacks full of animals, Charles brought back to the ship mounds of rocks, fossils, and minerals. In his personal notes, he wrote a lengthy entry comparing the pleasures of studying geology to the exhilaration of gambling. Often, he could hardly sleep at night because he was thinking of the day's geology.

The HMS Beagle *in the Strait of Magellan*

Engravings depicting the Beagle's *stop at Fort Desire*

SIX

Flycatcher to Scientist
1833-1835

Within a short amount of time, the *Beagle* was bursting with Darwin's samples. Even though special drawers had been built for Darwin, he still ran out of room. Captain FitzRoy and the crew commented, with a mixture of disgust and bewilderment, at the never-ending piles of apparent rubbish that Darwin kept dragging on board. The crew nicknamed him "the Flycatcher" as a joking tribute to his zealous methods. He was also called "the Philosopher" because of his detailed reflections about the mysteries of the natural world.

Charles patiently sorted through the heaps of samples, recorded information about where he had found them, labeled them, packed them, and sent them off on any vessel bound for England. There the specimens would be examined by experts. One shipment to Henslow included four barrels of animal corpses, skins, pickled fish, beetles in pill boxes, and rocks. Onlookers, astounded at Darwin's effort, remarked that he appeared intent on placing the entire continent of South America in specimen bottles.

Whenever he was not bottling and labeling specimens, Charles was writing about his findings. His notes and observations were filled with minute details. As a result of his work, the voyage of the *Beagle* was one of the most well-documented expeditions of its era.

In South America, Charles enjoyed trudging through jungle and grasslands or scaling high mountains on his own. Frequently, he had Captain FitzRoy drop him off at shore so that he could undertake long overland expeditions. He was so confident in his abilities that he often made arrangements for Captain FitzRoy to pick him up at a point 100 miles down

Charles finds a vampire bat biting a horse during one of his stops in Brazil.

the coast from where he had been let off. Darwin bravely confronted a variety of dangers. In Argentina he once found his path blocked by a bitter civil war. Rather than turn back, Darwin negotiated with the generals, gained passage through the war-torn territory, and collected what he needed.

His exceptional strength, courage, and endurance — along with his agreeable nature — won him the admiration of the crew. Thus, he was spared from the usual scorn that sailors usually showed toward "landlubbers" and "philosophers" on their ships. In fact, Darwin frequently proved that he was the fittest man aboard. In 1832 the *Beagle* made its first stop at Tierra del Fuego, the mountainous islands off the southern coast of South America. Darwin was warned against climbing some of the more dangerous peaks, particularly one on which a previous exploring party had lost two men. Darwin decided to climb the mountain despite the warning and made it to the top by himself.

On another occasion, Captain FitzRoy decided to leave the ship and do some exploring of his own. Along with Darwin and four other men, he rowed to shore and set off on a long hike over a dry, barren section of land. Late in the day, the heat grew unbearable, and the group had very little water remaining in their canteens. They were miles inland, in grave danger of dehydrating.

Off in the distance, they spotted what appeared to be a lake. Darwin and one other man walked onward to bring back fresh water for the group. But shortly before they reached the "lake," Darwin realized that there was no water at all. The lake was simply a mirage, a large bed of salt. The two men trudged back to the group with the bad news. Since most of them were in no shape to hike to the boat, Darwin and another man set off by themselves. They found their way back to the coast and dispatched a party to rescue the others. While the others suffered severe dehydration, Darwin was merely bedridden with a fever for two days.

These types of exploits, though, grew rarer as Charles began to lose enthusiasm for the physical part of his work. He had contracted a serious illness from an insect bite and became so ill that he needed seven weeks in bed to recover his strength. But mostly, hunting began to interfere with his new love, geology. After two years of shooting nearly all of the animals for his collection, he began to turn over the task to a crew member whom he had hired as a personal servant.

Charles showed an uncanny ability to make connections between what he saw and what he read. For example, when he found the bones of a giant sloth, he was able to recognize that he had found solid evidence of one of Lyell's theories proposed in *Principles of Geology*. Charles made an even more valuable discovery. The bones of this extinct sloth were scattered among fossils of a species of shellfish that still existed. The shellfish had obviously lived through the period of the sloth's decline, so there could not have been a catastrophe and a recreation. Charles and his servant dug the fossils out. Certainly, Charles thought, this disputed the theory that extinction of animals was caused by great global floods or similar catastrophes.

Throughout the voyage, Charles looked at other fossil remains and found many extinct life forms that resembled certain living animals of the area. Giant sloths resembled modern sloths, giant llamas resembled modern llamas, and certain other fossils resembled modern armadillos. Charles could not help but wonder why. Was there some reason these fantastic prehistoric creatures and their less-imposing counterparts in the modern world looked so much alike?

Engravings of fossil shells found by Charles on the voyage of the Beagle

In Argentina, Charles unearthed the skeleton of a horse. It had lived before some seashells found in the layer of rock above. But, supposedly, horses were first brought to the Americas by Spanish conquistadors only a few hundred years before. What did this discovery mean? Was it a clue as to why certain species appeared and disappeared over time?

After the *Beagle* sailed through the treacherous Strait of Magellan at the southern tip of South America in 1834, Charles went ashore by himself. While lying in a forest, he felt the ground beneath him rumble, and then the whole

Fuegans, the indigenous people of Tierra del Fuego, at a cove in the Beagle Canal

earth seemed to shudder. He was experiencing a violent earthquake, and he noted with awe and horror the devastation that it caused. Soon after, on an excursion near the ocean, he noticed stranded beds of mussel shells now uplifted and rotting on rocks. He recognized this as more proof favoring Lyell's radical theories.

When Charles discovered a petrified forest at 7,000 feet above sea level, he again saw the relationship between the discovery and the story it told about the earth. He was gathering evidence that the earth's crust was unstable. This evidence also seemed to support Lyell's notions of the earth's age.

Most of Charles's thinking at this time was focused on geology and Lyell's theories. In the meantime, Charles continued to compile lists of which forms of life were found where. While taking inventory of the plant life in South America, he noticed several odd patterns. For example, the same types of plants were repeatedly found in the same types of places, with one glaring exception. Vegetation growing east of the Andes Mountains was vastly different from that growing west of the mountains—even when the growing conditions were practically identical. Again, Charles suspected that such information contained a clue as to how different species adapted to their surroundings. Charles was not one to jump to conclusions, however. While he may have formed suspicions about evolution, he resisted forming strong opinions. For the most part, Charles simply asked himself questions and collected as much information as he could, hoping that those questions might someday be answered.

By the time the *Beagle* set sail for the Galapagos Islands in September 1835, Charles Darwin was a seasoned observer of nature. Experience and effort had helped hone his skills, and he would eventually become one of the most insightful biologists of all time.

One of the stony, barren islands of the Galapagos

SEVEN

The Galapagos and On
1835-1836

To a crew that had been at sea for more than three and a half years, already longer than they had planned, the Galapagos Islands—lying about 600 miles off the coast of Ecuador—must have been a most unwelcome detour on the way to Australia. As Charles described them, the islands looked as though God had caused it to rain stones. Black and forbidding, they were named after the huge tortoises that lived on the island.

At first glance, the islands appeared to be almost devoid of life. There were no mammals whatsoever, but the islands were dominated by the tortoises and lizards. Large cacti and a few leafless shrubs were the only plants hardy enough to exist on the rocks. There could be little for a naturalist to study. But as Charles set about taking samples of the creatures and plants, he discovered far more on the islands than he had expected.

These barren chunks of rock turned out to be home to at least 185 different varieties of plants. Even more intriguing, 100 of these were varieties that Charles had neither

An iguana

read about nor seen before. Animal life existed in the same extraordinary variety. Charles quickly noticed that the birds differed from all those he had seen on the South American mainland. He discovered 25 new species of birds and more than a dozen new types of fish. Even the tortoises and lizards differed markedly from tortoises and lizards in other parts of the world.

Charles realized that in these bleak volcanic islands he had stumbled upon a living laboratory. The Galapagos were small enough and isolated enough for him to study a very large part of their entire living communities—a task that would have been impossibly complex on any larger piece of land. Perhaps these islands would provide some insights into the history of plant and animal species.

Charles met a man who was very familiar with the islands. This man told Charles that the tortoises were so

A tortoise on one of the Galapagos Islands

distinctive that he could easily identify which of the 13 major Galapagos islands one was from. Tortoises with thick shells came from one island, smaller tortoises from another, round-shelled tortoises from yet another. Charles realized that some of the other types of life were also found only on one island or another.

Belatedly, Charles realized that he had been making a crucial mistake. Except for the mockingbirds, he had been lumping together all the samples from the various islands in one group as he organized his collections. He had been so intrigued by the differences between Galapagos plants and animals and those of the mainland that he had overlooked

Charles measures the speed of an elephant tortoise on one of the Galapagos islands.

the even more striking differences between the inhabitants of one island from another.

Here were numerous islands, packed closely together in this isolated ocean spot. Their climates, therefore, were identical. The islands were all formed from the same type of black rock. According to every known principle, the islands should have had virtually identical creatures and plants. As Charles separated his samples according to where he found them, he discovered that each island had its own distinct species of plants and animals. When the *Beagle* left the Galapagos Islands, Charles was still stumped.

Upon leaving the Galapagos, the *Beagle* sailed across the Pacific Ocean. Except for the task of circling the globe, their mission was largely complete, and the crew spent far less time surveying and sampling than they had in South America. A well-seasoned veteran of research by this time, Charles still managed to come up with several interesting discoveries. While in Tahiti, Australia, and New Zealand, he observed the same subtle differences among separated species that he had seen in the Galapagos. In countries oceans apart, he found many different variations of the same types of plants and animals. He still managed to fit in some geology research by studying coral reefs in the South Pacific Ocean.

When the *Beagle* reached the Cape Verde Islands off the west coast of Africa, Charles expected to find a situation similar to what he had seen in Galapagos. After all, here was another group of islands off the coast of a major continent.

This, however, was not the case. Life on the Cape Verde Islands resembled life on the African continent far more closely than it resembled life on the Galapagos Islands. Reorganizing his notes late in the voyage, Charles observed that, for all their distinctiveness, the living things on the

Galapagos Islands had been somewhat similar to those on the South American continent. Somehow life on the islands was related to life on the nearest continent, regardless of differences between the islands and the continent in climate and terrain. Why?

While the *Beagle* was at sea, Charles brooded on the problem. According to the accepted doctrines of both science and religion, the only answer to this puzzle of Galapagos could be that, when God created the world, God had singled out each of the Galapagos Islands and given each a unique assortment of life. God had specially designed these forms of life to be very similar to forms of life on the South American mainland.

Charles knew that he wanted to see if the evidence supported such a shaky explanation, so he started at the beginning. The Galapagos Islands had been formed in the ocean by volcanic eruptions. Taking into account Lyell's ideas about the earth being ancient and constantly changing, Charles thought the islands were probably formed more recently than the mainland. If that were true, he thought, then the islands had been populated more recently than the mainland. That meant that if the Galapagos creatures had been created in the same form and in the same places as they were now, a separate creation of those species had taken place after the original creation on the mainland.

If a separate creation had placed life on the islands, then why did the new species appear to be related to the species on the nearest continent? After all, the rocky Galapagos Islands, cooled by an ocean current, had a much different climate from the steamy, less rocky mainland of South America. Why should the two places have similar species?

Perhaps the answer was migration. Birds could have flown through the air, seeds could have been blown, and other seeds and animals from the mainland could have drifted over on the ocean currents to populate the previously barren islands. But then shouldn't the species on the islands be the same as those on the mainland?

Why did each island have separate species? Charles could understand if one island had lizards, another turtles, another finches, or some combination. That would have shown that a certain kind of animal had migrated to one island and not the other. But why would each island have its own species of tortoises, lizards, and finches? And why would these species be different from those found in other parts of the world?

Charles had no idea how or why such variation occurred, especially between two islands whose features were identical. At this point, he had no plan to use the information he had discovered to form a theory that would support the radical idea of evolution. But Charles's discoveries on Galapagos had certainly raised questions in his mind. Although he hoped that his many notebooks filled with data and observations might be of some use to someone, he was by no means confident that they would lead to anything important.

As excited as he was by his discoveries in the natural world, Charles was more than ready to be home by 1836. His seasickness continually plagued him, and the periods of homesickness grew longer and more painful. "I hate every wave of the ocean," he wrote home during the last year of his voyage. Finally, on October 2, 1836, nearly five years after leaving England, the *Beagle* arrived home.

The crowded, bustling streets of the city of London, with St. Paul's Cathedral in the background

EIGHT

The Beginnings of a Theory

1836-1838

There could be no doubt that the voyage aboard the *Beagle* had changed Charles Darwin. The packages he had sent to Henslow earned him a reputation among the British scientific community as an energetic, dedicated scientist. When first reunited with his son, Robert Darwin was so astounded by the physical changes in Charles that he exclaimed: "Why, the shape of his head is quite altered!"

So relieved was Charles to return to familiar surroundings that he temporarily escaped the consuming passion of his scientific work. He knew that, unless it was cataloged, the enormous collection he had built in South America was useless. If Charles wanted to find the secrets that all those fossils and specimens contained, he would have to find experts to name them. To be close to the geologists, zoologists, and botanists of England, he would take up residence in "dirty, odious" London, where his collection was stored. Because he had spent the past five years in wide open spaces,

Back in London, Charles spent countless hours watching the animals at the Zoological Gardens in Regent's Park.

the city made him feel as though he were caged.

The joy of returning home after so many years at sea and the headaches of sorting through all his samples sidetracked Charles only temporarily. In early 1837 he began to consider in earnest the questions his observations had raised.

Eventually, Charles spotted a trend in his vast collection. In South America, he had expected to find the same types of plants west of the Andes Mountains that he had found under similar climatic conditions on the east side. That had not been the case. Similarly, the Galapagos Islands were virtually identical to each other in climate, yet they were home to different species. What similarities were there between the islands and the areas on either side of the Andes?

The answer was isolation. The plants and animals east of the Andes had been isolated from plants and animals west of the Andes by an impassable barrier—the mountains. The plants and animals on each island were isolated from each other by water. Because of the almost total absence of wind in the Galapagos, the air didn't carry anything from one island to another.

The more Charles studied his notes, the more he realized that there was a direct relationship between isolation and the amount of variation between related species. The evidence seemed to indicate that there was greater variation among related animals that were separated by natural barriers than among related animals that could interbreed.

According to the commonly held view of nature, all species on earth remained unchanged from the day they were created until the end of time. If this were true, natural barriers should not have any effect on the variety of species. Could the traditional view be wrong?

Charles had already come to agree with Lyell that the geological formation of the earth was constantly changing. Could it be that Lamarck and others had been right—that species of plants and animals were constantly changing as well?

In the case of the Galapagos Islands, Charles thought that perhaps a few plants and animals had made their way to the islands. Could they have adapted somehow to their new surroundings? Perhaps the plants and animals that landed on separate islands each adapted in a different way. Couldn't that account for the variation between the species of the various islands?

In July 1837, Charles secretly started a notebook on the transmutation—the ability to change features—of species. Careful to avoid committing himself to one hypothesis too early, as he felt his grandfather and Lamarck did, Charles simply began to search through his records of South American geology and natural history, looking for evidence of transmutation. Charles realized that scientists had no solid definition of what a species was. In the 18th century, Carolus Linnaeus had created a system to classify all plants and animals. His system divided all living things into groups based on physical features and habits. The smallest of these groups—the one that could not be divided—was the "species," from the Latin word for "kind" or "type." Charles noticed, though, that it was often difficult to decide whether two creatures were two different species or just two varieties of one species that appeared different—in the same ways that two people look different from each other.

For his use, Charles eventually defined species as a group whose members can all interbreed—or reproduce— with one another. If two specimens appeared very similar but could not interbreed, then they would be considered different species.

There was reason to believe that these interbreeding members could change. English dog breeders had been able to produce a variety of breeds with widely differing characteristics. The bulldog, with its strength and tenacity, had been produced from the same species that also fostered the speedy greyhound. Expert breeders were able to produce dogs, horses, pigeons, and even plants with desirable traits. Surely that indicated that organisms had the ability to change, at least within a species. Charles even discovered a pattern that indicated a species could change so much that its members were unable to interbreed with the original species.

First, he recalled the uncanny resemblance between the fossils of certain extinct animals and skeletons of living animals. Modern armadillos very closely resembled the larger creatures that had since disappeared. Charles saw so many instances of this phenomenon that he could argue that some modern forms were successful adaptations of creatures that had been unable to survive environmental changes.

Second, Charles noted that as he had traveled south across South America, certain species of plants and animals were replaced by very similar species. For example, he noticed that the small Petise ostrich was replaced by a similar but larger ostrich. Despite their similarities, the two ostriches did not live in the same area. Lyell had suggested that species could be eliminated by competition with more successful rivals. Charles thought one way a rival would become more

Sketches of four different types of finches found on the Galapagos Islands. Only at this point did Charles begin to understand that they were different species.

A member of one of the unique varieties of tortoises found on the Galapagos Islands

successful would be to improve its ability to compete. Improvement was a form of change.

Third, the strange situation in the Galapagos Islands, when viewed in the light of these other observations, became clearer. These isolated islands had a unique variety of life, similar to that of the nearest continent. Why were they like mainland life despite the great differences in climate and land formation? The creatures and plants on the Galapagos must have come from the mainland.

How could isolation create variety, as it seemed to do among the separate islands and among creatures divided by the Andes Mountains? It could only do so if the species were changing. Isolation allowed for one group of a species to adapt to its particular environment, while another adapted differently because of its different environment.

When the animals or plants lived in large groups, these new characteristics became intermixed. That kept the group changing together. The characteristics of isolated animals never intermixed with those of the larger group. As time went on, the traits of isolated plants and animals gradually became more pronounced until eventually they were quite different from the original group.

The differences between the ostriches could be explained in this way: Two groups of the original ostrich species had migrated in different directions and become isolated. Each evolved some adaptations that gave it an advantage over the other when the territories of the two collided.

Charles's explanation of evolution, then, differed from Lamarck's. Lamarck saw direct lines of evolution. He believed that life evolved in continuing patterns from simple to complex. Charles believed that evolution tended to progress from simple to complex, but these changes did not necessarily follow a straight line. A number of different species could branch off in different directions from the original.

Despite the evidence he had collected, Charles was not at all satisfied that he had discovered anything important. Although the evidence seemed to indicate that species could change, and that it may have happened, there was nothing that explained how individual organisms changed.

Lamarck had theorized that animals deliberately tried to develop certain physical features to better cope with their environment. But Charles quickly discarded Lamarck's notion. Wind, rain, heat, and so on could not cause birds to change color nor lengthen their beaks. Neither was it at all reasonable to suppose that organisms could produce these changes by willpower.

Charles pored over his notes and enlisted the help of all

Charles kept quite a variety of pigeons—shown here are an English carrier, a short-faced English tumbler, an English barb,

kinds of experts in his search for an answer. He consulted with zoologists, botanists, geologists, gardeners, and animal breeders. In his usual tenacious, plodding way, Charles pieced together evidence that drew him closer to an answer.

He learned that the secret of successful animal breeding was to select desirable variations among all the variations that naturally occurred among members of the species. If a breeder were interested in speed, he or she would mate those animals that displayed the greatest speed. Over time, the continual favoring of animals built for speed would result in generations for which speed would be a standard feature rather than an exceptional one.

Charles thought that this same process of selection must also account for the differences within species in nature. He wondered, since people certainly were not involved in selecting which traits were to survive in a species, who or what was? After 15 months of study, he still had not solved that mystery.

and an English fantail—and he was astonished by the diversity among them.

For the next two years, Charles worked as feverishly as he had aboard the *Beagle*. He wrote countless letters and made numerous visits asking for help, advice, or further information. Slowly he was able to sift through the mountain of samples he had collected in South America.

At the same time, he finished organizing and rewriting the notes in his daily log. Portions of his journal had been published as part of Captain FitzRoy's narrative of the voyage, which was released shortly after the *Beagle* returned. John Murray, a publisher, was impressed by Charles's ability to describe unusual sights and ideas so clearly. He urged Charles to work up his own narrative of what had become a very famous voyage.

Charles agreed to try. He wanted to write in such a way that the style was transparently clear. The result was a book published in 1839, now known as *A Naturalist's Voyage on the Beagle*, one of the most popular and readable accounts ever written about an exploration.

Charles discovered that his newly acquired success and popularity brought with it some uncomfortable side effects. He began to chafe under the numerous requests asking him to write for publications or make presentations, or to undertake duties for various scientific societies. Although he was honored to be offered the post of secretary to the Geological Society, he worried about the time this would take away from his work. In the end, he accepted the job reluctantly, although he never felt comfortable in the position.

Charles was a notoriously poor public speaker. He was so acutely aware of this shortcoming that, by the time he was 30, any kind of public appearance caused him great distress. Headaches, nausea, weakness, dizziness, insomnia, and irregular heartbeats appeared so frequently that Charles began to avoid such stressful situations.

In September 1838, Charles read *An Essay on the Principle of Population*, written by Thomas Malthus 40 years earlier. Malthus pointed out that all forms of life produce far more offspring than is necessary to maintain a constant level of population. If even a small percentage of all newborn robins, rabbits, mice, foxes, and other animals were to survive, the world would be quickly overrun.

Malthus argued that populations are kept in balance by competing for a limited amount of space, food, and other resources. All living things, according to Malthus, are engaged in a "struggle for existence." Out of the vast pool of living things brought into the world, only the fittest are able to survive.

Although the gentle Charles disliked the way Malthus applied his "survival of the fittest" doctrine to human societies, he saw that this was the element that had been missing from his theory of evolution. Because of incredibly high fer-

Malthus observed that population tends to increase more rapidly than the food supply. Here, in crowded London, beggars line the streets. Malthus suggested to Darwin the relationship between progress and the survival of the fittest.

tility rates, a vast pool of all living things struggled for available resources. Change occurred all the time, because nature provided an almost limitless assortment of inherited variations. Out of the millions of humans who had ever lived, few had exactly the same features.

Here, in the only known photo of Charles with a member of his family, are Charles and his eldest son, William, in 1842.

NINE

Settling Down
1838-1858

Comparing his life to those of his friends, Charles was lonely, and he wanted to get married. He was attracted to his cousin, Emma Wedgwood. He knew her well and could hardly have imagined a better bride. Emma was the same age as he, was intelligent, uncommonly cheerful, and a sympathetic listener. Whereas Charles floundered hopelessly in foreign languages, Emma could speak fluent French, Italian, and German. She was quick and talented, skilled at a wide variety of activities including needlework, archery, and skating.

Charles suspected that he could hardly be expected to attract a woman such as Emma. It took all the courage he could muster to ask Emma on November 11, 1838, if she would marry him.

To his surprise, Emma readily agreed. She was impressed by his open, honest nature, and was touched by his gentle, affectionate manner. Unknown to Charles, he also had some behind-the-scenes help from the other Wedgwood cousins. They had thought for a long time that the two would be a good match and had done their best to smooth things

Emma Darwin, age 31, at the time of her marriage to Charles

along. After a short engagement, Charles and Emma were married on January 29, 1839, and moved to what both agreed was an ugly house in London.

Shortly after his wedding, Charles made one of his frequent visits to Charles Lyell. During their conversation they discussed the coral reefs that Darwin had studied in the South Pacific. Lyell had puzzled over the origins of coral reefs and had decided that they came from volcanic craters. Darwin disagreed. He argued that the coral was built by sea organisms. Lyell asked how Darwin could explain why coral was frequently found in deep water, where these organisms did not thrive. Darwin proposed that while the organisms were building upward, the ocean floor had been sinking.

Although this explanation totally contradicted a theory of Lyell's, he immediately saw the wisdom of Darwin's explanation. Instead of growing defensive, Lyell actually danced for joy that Darwin had uncovered a better theory. Furthermore, from his conversations with the geologist, Charles discovered that Lyell was not as hostile to the idea of evolution as he had thought from reading Lyell's book.

With Lyell as an example, Charles began reconsidering the unthinkable. Was there any chance that the old species had evolved into new species?

Although Charles had pieced together most of this information by 1839, he still stubbornly resisted forming his observations into a theory. He was determined to keep an open mind until he was certain there was enough data to support a particular view. It would not be until 1842 that he even allowed himself to sketch an outline of the concept that species had not been created separately but had evolved, becoming more advanced, by the process of natural selection. In 1844 he expanded his initial 44-page draft into a 230-page paper.

The newlywed Charles enjoyed going to parties and dinners. But like everything else in his life, those pleasures took a back seat to his zeal for science. In addition, the heart condition that had threatened to prevent him from joining the *Beagle* seemed to have returned. There were few outward signs that anything was wrong with Charles. Friends and relatives often remarked on how well he looked.

Charles sought out many prominent physicians, including his father. But no physical cause was found for Charles's illness, and although many creative cures were tried, none of them proved effective.

Meantime, Charles's fascination with science was reaching fanatical proportions. He observed that he had become incapable of finding pleasure in anything but grinding general laws out of large collections of facts. He mourned the fact that subjects that had once fascinated him had lost their appeal. The poetry of Milton, Shelley, and Byron, and the plays of Shakespeare had once given him great pleasure. Music and paintings had provided him with many hours of enjoyment and relaxation in his younger years. But as he delved deeper into his research, he was bored by even a single verse of poetry. Beautiful art no longer captivated him. And the man who had once shouted in ecstasy over the incredible scenery of the Brazilian forest no longer found the same satisfaction in scenic beauty of any kind.

He always referred to poetry, literature, and music as higher forms of intellect than science. "Loss of these tastes is the loss of happiness," he once said, adding that such loss was also "injurious to moral character and possibly even intellect." He was addicted to the pursuit of science. "I seem to have become a withered leaf for every subject but science."

Charles and Emma's first child, William, was born on December 27, 1839, the eighth anniversary of his father's departure aboard the *Beagle*. Although Charles was as proud as any new parent and was a kind, caring father, he frequently slipped into the habit of regarding William as a fresh subject of natural history. The baby had scarcely been born before Charles opened his notebook and began recording his observations of the baby's expressions—when they were used and what emotions they seemed to represent. Charles also studied when the child began to display various movements.

By now, almost any type of activity that was not related to his research made Charles physically ill. His discomfort at dinner parties became so acute that he gradually gave them up altogether. Meetings were such a hardship for him that he avoided them whenever possible. Before long even friendly visits from casual or professional acquaintances left him sleepless or shivering uncontrollably.

Outdoor activities taxed him beyond his endurance. In the summer of 1842, Charles went out one last time on a tour of the rugged countryside of North Wales. Never again did he venture into the wilderness. Incredibly, the man who a few years earlier had outhiked an entire ship's crew had, at the age of 33, grown too weak to even take a long walk.

Charles and Emma decided that they needed to find a quiet country home more like where they had been raised, away from society. Emma disliked city life as much as Charles did, so they began to look in earnest for a way out of the bustle of the city. Unfortunately, Charles's work required that he consult frequently with experts in London.

For many months the Darwins searched for a quiet, secluded house near the city. After a long and futile effort, they realized that they could not afford to be choosy. In September 1842, Charles, Emma, and William moved into a house on 18 acres of land near the village of Down in Kent. Although the property was only 16 miles from London, it was tucked away in a section of woods far from the main roads. There was not even a railroad station in Down.

The house was large and spacious—and more expensive than they could afford. But Robert Darwin provided the down payment, and the large yearly allowance that Emma received from her father took care of the day-to-day expenses.

Although the solitude of the country did make life more

A sketch of Down House from the garden. Charles spent hours

pleasant for the Darwins, Charles's health continued to decline. Charles scaled back his activities until he was doing
practically nothing. By 1843 Charles restricted himself to
meeting with only the few friends and colleagues with whom
he felt most comfortable, such as Charles Lyell, Joseph
Hooker, and Thomas Huxley.

The few activities that he kept up were rigidly sched-
uled, never varying from one day to the next. The early

sitting on the porch, thinking through the idea of evolution.

morning period from 8:00 to 9:30 was his most productive, and he usually worked an hour or so later in the day as well.

Several times a day, Charles took his walking stick out to what he called his Sandwalk and did slow laps around a short track. Charles had created the Sandwalk by planting a long strip of maples, oaks, elms, lime trees, and shrubs on one end of his property. Then he had sand brought in from a nearby pit and poured around the strip. He had a pile of stones set up on one side of the path when he started his walk. Each time he passed that point he kicked off one of the stones, which saved him the trouble of keeping track of how many rounds he had gone. Day after day, Charles made his rounds of the Sandwalk.

In comparison with the rest of his day, evenings were more social. After supper, Charles would play backgammon with Emma. True to form, he kept a running score of their games throughout the years. Then he would lie down on the couch and listen to Emma play the piano. In place of his former love of literature, he read popular novels and newspapers. Because he occasionally did not have even the strength to hold a book, Charles sometimes had the books torn into more manageable pieces. When he lacked the strength for that, he enjoyed having someone read to him.

From left to right: *William, born in 1839; Annie, born in 1841;*

Ironically, Charles generally rested far less at night than he did during the day. His pain and nausea reached its peak during evenings. Charles once remarked that he had not slept through an entire night in three years without waking from severe stomach pain.

Charles's sufferings dominated his household. His sickness was considered a normal, everyday circumstance that was part of the family routine. Good health was an exception. Somehow Emma managed to find the time and emotional strength to nurse her husband's never-ending illness while at the same time catering to the needs of their children. Emma would eventually give birth to ten children.

Charles's sufferings did not affect his work. Even on days when he was too ill to do anything else, he still managed to find the energy to write in his notebooks. Charles

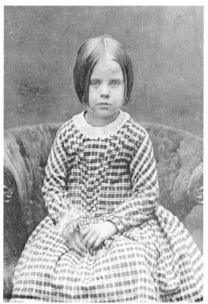

Henrietta, born in 1843; and George, born in 1845.

even claimed that working on his theories was therapy. He wrote that this work made him "for a time forget my daily discomfort."

His mind was rarely occupied with any concerns except his research. Because of the pains that kept him awake most

Elizabeth, the Darwins' youngest daughter and sixth of ten children, was born in 1847 and was quiet, nervous, and dependent.

Charles's study in Down House

of the night, Charles had long stretches of uninterrupted time to think over his latest theories. He was accomplishing more than most healthy, energetic people accomplish in a lifetime, as he put together a theory that would shake western civilization to its roots.

Charles, however, did not go public with his ideas for 20 years, and even then it was not out of choice. Some of this delay was due to his cautious, thorough nature. Ever mindful of Grandfather Erasmus's reputation for playing fast and loose with the facts, Charles was determined not to get caught without evidence to back up his theories. He continued to stockpile mounds of evidence in support of his ideas.

Charles could foresee the uproar his paper would cause. He had always hated controversy. His delicate health made it ever more essential that he avoid upsetting situations. Charles had probed the minds of enough English biologists to know that opinion was solidly in favor of unchangeable species. He also had seen, first-hand, what the scientific community would do to someone whose ideas were unacceptable. Once he had been present at a society meeting during which a controversial paper had been read. Later he had discovered that all mention of that paper had been censored from the society's minutes.

Then in 1844, a book called *The Vestiges of the Natural History of Creation* was published by an anonymous author. This book argued that the fossil record showed clear support that all of nature was in a continual state of change. The book created a scandal. In view of all this, Charles was reluctant to go public with his findings until the scientific community was more receptive to the idea of evolution. At first he told only his wife about his theory. She feared for his soul, which could not have eased any guilt he felt. In 1844 he finally alluded to his theory to trusted friends such as Lyell and Joseph Hooker. Writing to Hooker in 1844, Charles admitted that describing his theory of evolution was "like confessing murder."

For a number of years during the 1850s, Charles seemed to abandon his probings into the origin of species. Instead he immersed himself in a long and involved study of the sea creatures known as barnacles. As usual Charles plunged into his latest interest as if it were the only thing in the world worth doing. His children grew so used to watching him

The Darwin family at home about 1863, from left to right, *Leonard, Henrietta, Horace, Emma, Elizabeth, Francis, and a visitor*

dissect the marine creatures that one of them, upon visiting a friend's house, asked to see where the friend's father "did his barnacles." Charles later admitted that his four-volume study of barnacles was probably not worth the eight years he spent on it.

In 1856, Lyell finally prodded Charles into writing out his evolutionary theories in greater detail. While Charles was doing so, a letter arrived that gave him the shock of his life and finally forced him to go public.

Charles Darwin at age 45

TEN

The Secret Is Out

1857-1867

Charles, who was diligent at corresponding with other scientists, had also been communicating with Alfred Russell Wallace. Wallace had some ideas that were similar to those of Darwin. On June 18, 1858, Darwin received a letter from Wallace. While lying sick with malaria in the jungles of Malaysia, Wallace had come up with the idea that natural selection was the driving force behind evolution. Within a week, Wallace had worked out most of the details that Darwin had taken years of research to discover. A stunned Charles wrote that if Wallace had Darwin's manuscript in 1842, he could not have made a better summary. Totally unaware of Darwin's effort, Wallace had eagerly asked Darwin to forward the letter to Lyell if he thought the ideas good enough. The letter could not have come at a worse time. Charles and Emma's youngest son, Charles Waring, was stricken with scarlet fever on June 23 and died a few days later. The grief-stricken father was in no condition to deal with the fact that after 20 years of research, someone else had come up with the same theory.

Charles immediately began writing a letter to Wallace in which he surrendered all claims to the theories that Wallace had described. As he told his friends, he would rather burn the whole book than have it thought that he behaved in a paltry spirit. Charles could not bring himself to finish the letter, though. Too distraught over his family and this latest news, he simply forwarded Wallace's letter to Lyell, along with his recommendation. He told Lyell he did not care what happened next. If Wallace wanted to publish his ideas, as he had every right to do, Charles was willing to give up all ownership of his theory.

Fortunately for Charles, his friends came up with an idea that allowed him recognition for his theory, while also maintaining his integrity. Joseph Hooker and Charles Lyell

Sir Joseph Hooker

Sir Charles Lyell

arranged for papers by both Darwin and Wallace to be presented to the Linnean Society of London. These papers were then to be published in the society's journal. Wallace, every bit the gentleman Darwin was, further smoothed tensions by referring to the theory as "Darwinism." Never did he seek credit for his ideas, trusting that Darwin had indeed gotten there first.

The crisis between Darwin and Wallace must have seemed like a lot of fuss over nothing when their papers were virtually ignored by the scientific community. The shortened version of the theory, as presented in the joint papers to the Linnean Society, struck most observers as a familiar mixture of old facts and new speculation.

After 13 months and 10 days of solid effort, Charles finally completed a short version of the manuscript he had been writing for many years. John Murray had agreed to publish it. After the cool reception the joint papers had received, Charles did not expect that his book would sell. Feeling guilty about the loss Murray was about to experience, Charles assured Murray that he should feel no obligation to publish the manuscript if he thought it would cause him financial hardship. At the very least, Charles thought Murray should scale back his plan to print 1,250 copies.

Murray thought otherwise. On November 11, 1859, *On the Origin of Species by Means of Natural Selection, or the Preservation of Favoured Races in the Struggle for Life* rolled off the press. Within a few hours, the book was sold out. Two months later a second edition of 3,000 copies was published, soon to be devoured by the public. Newspapers and magazines, however, paid little attention to the book until they discovered that Darwin's theory challenged teachings of the church. The idea of natural selection seemed to show that God was not in charge—that all of life was basically an accident. And the theory seemed to imply that humans might have come from lower forms of life, such as apes. People in 19th-century England considered the idea of evolution demeaning to humanity and contrary to the teachings of the Bible. Charles's theory was quickly branded the "Ape Theory," because it implied that humans had evolved from apes. Far from being ignored, *The Origin of Species* sparked two reactions—astonishment and outrage.

The astonishment came from the scientific community. Darwin's explanation of natural selection was so easy to understand, lógical, and well-documented that many of the top scholars in the field were dumbfounded. Unlike the works of other brilliant scientists, there was nothing in *The Origin of Species* that an average, reasonably intelligent person could

"Darwin's bulldog," Thomas Huxley

not understand. What was more, Darwin had unearthed very few facts that were not previously known. Thomas Huxley, who defended Darwin's theory so vigorously that he became known as "Darwin's bulldog," was almost embarrassed that no one had pieced together the evolution/natural selection package earlier.

Most scholars were surprised that Darwin was the one who came up with the concrete theory of evolution. For despite his impressive performance aboard the *Beagle,* Darwin never showed the brilliance of many of his peers. He had been described as "tortoise-like in both thought and action."

An engraving of the gentle Charles walking on the grounds of Down House

By his own admission, he rarely could think quickly enough to hold his own in an argument and was hopeless at giving speeches. He was far more a professional student than a teacher, constantly seeking out the experts for information. With his limited formal training, he had less knowledge of the basics of biology than many.

Furthermore, while Darwin was admired for his great attention to detail, he retained many of the haphazard, unprofessional habits of a hobbyist. He never learned to sketch properly and later had some of his children illustrate his works. Darwin often fashioned his own clumsy instruments for research, and he occasionally accepted information from questionable sources. Rather than constructing a proper laboratory, he relied on a greenhouse in the back of the kitchen for his plant observations.

The outrage came from the rest of society. The most celebrated attack was launched by the Bishop of Oxford, who sarcastically asked Huxley whether he was descended from apes on his father's or his mother's side. In a famous reply, Huxley declared he could take more pride in being related to apes than in being related to a man who could do nothing more with his enormous talent than ridicule important scholarly contributions.

A number of people thought Darwin's theory signaled the end of civilization. They thought that only the belief in an ordered world under God's rule kept people from being savages. They felt that Darwin had "disproved" God's involvement in the world, and that this would remove all moral restraints from society.

The opponents of *The Origin of Species* were particularly frustrated that Darwin proved such a poor target for their wrath. Had he been a brash, outspoken character, they would have had an easy time focusing on him as an instrument of evil. Yet critics were left to rail at a gentle, kindly invalid. Despite the stress caused by his illness, no one could remember Darwin being irritable or impolite. Whenever he asked a favor of anyone, even of the youngest of his children, he preceded it with "would you be so kind." He was

A cartoonist's version of Darwinism: a young gent is humiliated by the appearance of his well-bred "forefather."

acknowledged by all to be exceedingly humble. In conversation, he invariably introduced his ideas by saying, "You will think this utter bosh, but..." He could never quite believe

Another cartoonist's version of Darwin with his "forefather"

that educated people considered his ideas important. When looking back at the books that he had written, Charles had difficulty comprehending that he had actually been the author.

Far from thinking himself infallible, Charles was quick to confess his mistakes. Once, in a paper, he had explained a certain land form as being caused by the action of the sea. When another geologist offered another explanation, Charles immediately saw that he was wrong. "My paper is one long, gigantic blunder," he said. On another occasion, a friend pointed out an error in an assumption that had been the basis of several weeks of Charles's research. Charles responded that he was the most miserable, bemuddled, stupid dog in all England!

Lyell, no stranger to criticism from an outraged public, had once advised Charles to have nothing to do with the controversies that his work might bring. Charles never uttered a public word in defense of his theories.

Generous of spirit even to his critics, he later wrote that he had "almost always been treated honestly" by his reviewers. Occasionally Charles would comment to a friend on some aspect of the debate. A common complaint was that if species changed as Darwin said, then why weren't fossils found from stages of the change, from one species to another. Charles wrote that he would be happy to show evidence of all those changes if someone could show him examples of every step between the bulldog and the greyhound.

For the most part, he ignored the criticism and went on to other things. Shortly after *The Origin of Species* was published, he noticed insects trapped by a sundew plant, and launched into a study of insectivorous plants. He also busied himself studying climbing plants and cross-pollination.

Not that he was indifferent to the distress his theories

would cause. Charles had wrestled at length with the problem of how to reconcile the idea of natural selection with his religious convictions. However, as he focused ever more narrowly on science, he was able to deal only with concrete facts, not with theology.

Eventually he gave up trying to figure out where religion fit into the whole scheme. He would stick to science, which was something he could comprehend. The subject of God, Charles decided, was beyond human understanding. "A dog might as well speculate on the mind of Newton," he said.

Charles had also been sensitive enough to controversy that he had done his best to compose *The Origin of Species* in a way that would not offend his family and friends. The word "evolution" was never mentioned in the book. Despite the claims of his critics, Charles avoided discussing the possible origins of humans in *The Origin of Species.*

By the time Charles took up the issue of how humans had come into existence, the public had grown weary of the debate. The publication of *The Descent of Man,* which theorized that humans were also the product of evolution rather than instantaneous creation, stirred up far less debate than had *The Origin of Species.*

Scientists had accepted Darwin's ideas as a useful tool in the study of living things. Theologians began to accept the idea that evolution had nothing to do with the beginnings of life—only with what has happened since the beginnings. Some began to understand natural selection as a divine tool rather than a proof against the existence of a divine being. The concept of evolution had changed the way many people thought, and yet civilization had not collapsed.

Charles sits on the front porch of his home in Down

∡ ELEVEN ⫫

The Legacy
1867–1882

Publication of *The Origin of Species* made Darwin the most famous scientist in Europe. Yet it had no visible effect on his life. Charles's routine and his illness continued unchanged. The last 40 years of his life were spent in carefully rationed bursts of work, romps with his children, and long periods of rest. His own obsession with the origins of life had robbed him of the comfort of arts or amusement, leaving the faithful attention of Emma as his only support against the constant pain and weariness.

In 1867 he wrote a short autobiography. Four years later, in 1871, the wedding of one of his daughters brought him out into public once more. Charles made an effort to attend the ceremony, held at a church just down the road from his house. But despite the fact that the service was short, Charles grew so uncomfortable and exhausted that he doubted his ability to survive it.

During the last years of his life, his disease seemed to improve slightly. The pains lessened, although they did not go away. On April 14, 1882, Charles was sitting at supper

*Emma Darwin
in 1881*

with his family when he suddenly felt ill. Attempting to reach the safety of his sofa, Charles fainted. For the next four days, the nausea and fatigue that had been his constant companion for over 40 years overwhelmed him. On April 19, he died, apparently of heart failure. Charles Darwin was buried in Westminster Abbey, almost within arm's length of another famous English scientist, Isaac Newton.

Charles once wrote that he never expected to do more than to show that there was another side to the question of the mutability of species. In his naive way, he simply was prying into questions in a way that no one before him had. Later on he summed up his work by saying that he had no doubt that much of what he had written in *The Origin of Species* would be proved false, but that he trusted the framework would hold up to examination.

*Charles Darwin
about 1880*

In the century since his death, Darwin's theories have been examined with a thoroughness and passion that is unique in the world of science. The brushfire of controversy set off by the publication of *The Origin of Species* has never been extinguished. Occasionally it smolders in hidden places, only to flare up again in intense debates over public school curriculum and in conflicts between religious groups.

Darwin's theories on the changeable nature of species and the evolution of life from simpler forms to complex forms through natural selection have been frequently debated, and occasionally modified. Yet they have remained the cornerstone of a science that attempts to answer the question: How did the earth come to be the way it is? For the most part, Charles's hopes and expectations for the work that literally consumed his life have so far been fulfilled.

Bibliography

Brent, Peter. *Charles Darwin: A Man of Enlarged Curiosity.* New York: Harper and Row, 1981.

Chancellor, John. *Charles Darwin.* New York: Taplinger, 1976.

Clark, Ronald W. *The Survival of Charles Darwin: A Biograph of a Man and an Idea.* New York: Random House, 1984.

Darwin, Charles. *Autobiography.* Edited by Nora Barlow. New York: Norton, 1969.

———. *Charles Darwin's Beagle Diary.* Edited by R. D. Keynes. Cambridge: Cambridge University Press, 1988.

———. *On the Origin of Species.* New York: The Modern Library, 1936.

———. *The Red Notebook of Charles Darwin.* Edited by Sandra Herbert. Ithaca: Cornell University Press, 1980.

Desmond, Adrian and James Moore. *Darwin: The Life of a Tormented Evolutionist.* New York: Warner, 1992.

Gould, Stephen Jay. *Ever Since Darwin: Reflections on Natural History.* New York: Norton, 1977.

Irvine, William. *Apes, Angels, and Victorians: The Story of Darwin, Huxley, and Evolution.* New York: McGraw-Hill, 1955.

Miller, Jonathan. *Darwin for Beginners.* New York: Pantheon, 1982.

Moore, Ruth E. *Charles Darwin: A Great Life in Brief.* New York: Knopf, 1955.

Patterson, Colin. *Evolution.* Ithaca: Cornell University Press, 1978.

Pickering, Sir George White. *Creative Malady.* New York: Oxford University Press, 1974.

Russell, A. J. *Their Religion.* London: Hodder and Stoughton, 1934.

Index

(Numbers in **bold face** refer to illustrations)

Photo Acknowledgments

112